# THE PARABLE
## OF THE
## FATHER'S HEART

# THE PARABLE OF THE FATHER'S HEART

### G. CAMPBELL MORGAN

**BAKER BOOK HOUSE**
Grand Rapids, Michigan 49506

PHOTOLITHOPRINTED BY CUSHING - MALLOY, INC.
ANN ARBOR, MICHIGAN, UNITED STATES OF AMERICA

# CONTENTS

# I

## The Far Country

*A certain man had two sons; and the younger of them
said to his father, Father, give me the portion of thy
substance that falleth to me. And he divided unto
them his living. And not many days after, the
younger son gathered all together, and took his journey into a far country.*—Luke xv.11-13a.*

THIS fifteenth chapter of Luke is a page peculiar to him, and contains the answer of
Jesus to a criticism of the Pharisees and scribes.
It opens with the declaration that "all the publicans and sinners were drawing near unto him
for to hear him," and that "the Pharisees and
the scribes murmured, saying, This man receiveth sinners, eateth with them." One of the
things that the religious rulers of Jesus' time
could not understand, and did not attempt to
understand, was the fact that He received, and

* This and the following texts are from the American
Standard Edition of the Revised Bible, copyright by the
International Council of Religious Education. Used by
permission.

[ 7 ]

sat down to eat with, sinning men in an ordinary way. In answer to that which troubled the moral teachers of His own day Jesus uttered the words of this entire chapter.

This answer of Jesus consists of one parable, not three. We generally say three parables, and there is a sense in which that is quite permissible: the man with the lost sheep, the woman and the lost piece of silver, and the prodigal son. All such description is correct if we remember that this is one set address, continuous, consecutive, complete. It is therefore really one parable with three facets. The inclusive truth taught in the parable is that of the place of lost things in the economy of God: a lost sheep, a lost piece of silver, the lost son. He showed in the entire parable how God acts in the presence of lost things. None of them is abandoned. All of them are valuable, and all of them are sought; and the way of the finding of all is revealed. This is the supreme value of the whole teaching. It shows us God's way of finding His lost things.

In the first phase of the parable the work of the Son is the supreme subject, the Shepherd who seeks and finds His sheep. In the second, the work of the Spirit is suggested by the woman who constantly sweeps the house until the lost silver is found. In the final phase of the parable the work of the Father is revealed. So in that answer of Jesus, in language which every child can understand, He set forth the fact of the Divine activity in the mystery of the threefold Personality in unity, in the presence of lost things.

I do not propose wholly to ignore the first two phases of the parable dealing finally with the shepherd work of Christ, the activating of the Church by the Spirit, and the inter-relation of the three. We will begin however where Jesus ended, for these are the fundamental things. We speak of this as the parable of the prodigal. In certain senses it may be true, but I think it is an unfortunate one. The root meaning of the word prodigal is one *driven forth*. That does not apply here, for this boy was not driven out. He went out. Or take the acquired meaning. We talk about a prodigal today, and we mean one who is lavish or extravagent in expenditure, and one given over to the more vulgar forms of sin. We have no proof that this young man was guilty of any of these things. I know he spent all in riotous living, but there is no proof that he was degraded. Indeed, I could argue that there was, in the very days of his darkness and misery, something fine about him. This man never lost his honor. "He would fain have been filled with the husks that the swine did eat; and no

[*9*]

man gave unto him." He did not steal. There is a touch of fine morality in that. We have not reached the point of the parable if we are seeing the power of God to deal with the "down and out." I love that slogan of the Salvation Army. "A man may be down, but he is never out." That is a great thing to remember as we go to seek and save the lost. But if we simply look here for a picture of such a man as vulgarized, and down and out, it is not here. I would also remind you that the word prodigal does not occur in the text. The Scripture speaks of him as "the younger son."

By referring to this as the parable of the prodigal son we lay emphasis on the wrong point, the wrong word, at the wrong place. The true emphasis is not on the boy, but on his father. It is an unveiling of the heart of God, and in all that it is intended to teach there is no more remarkable or beautiful passage in the Scriptures of truth. It is a revelation of the relation of man to God, of the true meaning and issue of man's separation from God, and supremely of the infinite grace and tenderness of the Father's heart.

In this meditation on the first phase of the story we see, first, the revealed relationship between man and God. "A certain man had two sons." Second, the way in which man has lost that relation, the way of separation, revealed in the opening sentences: "Father, give me the portion of substance that falleth to me. And he divided unto them his living. And not many days after the younger son gathered all together, and took his journey." Finally to where it leads, "the far country."

What is the relationship existing? "A certain man had two sons." Here we are brought face to face with the underlying fact of human life. The relationship between God and man is that man is a son of God. One is always conscious of the acute theologian who enjoys seeing if the preacher is orthodox. I am content to abide by the Book, and the revelation of the Book, and the truth as revealed in the Book. It may be argued Jesus said of the Jews, "Ye are of your father the devil." He certainly did, but how did they become children of the devil? Not by creation. The fundamental fact revealed here is that whatever is said about this younger son, he was the son of his father. That is the whole testimony of the Bible concerning human life. The story in Genesis sets the whole creation in relation to God. All creation depended on God's wisdom and power and fiat. In that ancient story of poetic suggestiveness and truth, we see that

[ *11* ]

before man appeared on the created scene there was counsel. "Let us make man in our image, after our likeness." It was by the Divine breath man became a living soul.

If in the ancient story we are immediately introduced to the fact of sin, and if through all the records of the past we find references to sin and death, it is nevertheless impossible to escape from the fact that man is a distinct creation of God. Everything essential to his being is divine in its origin. Such is the conception of the whole of the Old Testament. On that day in the dark period in the history of God's ancient people, when they had coined a false proverb, and were bandying it about as a cloak for their own wrongdoing, blaming their fathers for their sin, they said, "The fathers have eaten sour grapes, and the children's teeth are set on edge." That is untrue. It is a lie, often quoted today. It was dealt with very fully by the prophet Ezekiel. In answer to that false proverb he said, This is the truth, "all souls are mine; as the soul of the father, so also the soul of the son is mine; the soul that sinneth, it shall die." No man shall die for his father's sin. There is first-hand relationship between man and God.

Turning to the New Testament, we take one illustration from the Gospel stories. The

Gospel of Luke is peculiarly the Gospel of the humanity of our Lord, and the Gospel for humanity generally. Matthew was written for the Jew; Mark, perchance, for the Roman citizen; and John for the mystic and the believer. It is a significant fact that when Luke would tell the story of the Logos of Jesus—for that is what he called Him at the commencement of his writing —when dealing with His human nature, he inserted a genealogy, not that of the adoption of Jesus by Joseph, but that of the actual birth of Jesus through the line of Mary. Luke went back, sweeping through Abraham until he came to Adam, the first man. How did he end? "Adam, who was the son of God." There is a sense in which that applies to all the names in the long list of that genealogy, and of all men everywhere.

Paul, preaching on Mar's Hill, quoted from the Greek poets and verified the accuracy of their declaration, "being then the offspring of God." That is the fundamental truth here. We never understand the full and final significance of this great parable until we start there. The man presented to us here is the son of his father. Man is the offspring of God.

Yet perhaps the most flaming revelation of the truth is found in the letter to the Hebrews, almost accidentally and incidentally, so that we hurry over it and miss its profound significance. The writer of the letter says, "We had the fathers of our flesh to chasten us, and we gave them reverence; shall we not much rather be in subjection to the Father of spirits and live?" This is the Christian philosophy revealed. "The fathers of our flesh . . . the Father of spirits." No man is the father of the spirit of his child. He is the father only of the flesh. That is what Wordsworth meant, in spite of all criticism of him, when he said,

> "Trailing clouds of glory do we come
> From God who is our home."

It is when we see that truth about ourselves and humanity generally that we begin to understand what sin is. That is clearly revealed as we look at this picture which Jesus drew. The facts then revealed are these: Man is offspring of God. His being is due to the Divine action. Our being is His. Our likeness is His. Our possibilities are His. We have no power which He has not created. The only thing in us which He did not create is the paralysis which prevents the use of power. The only thing in us which He did not create is the poison which makes it impossible to come to realization of all the meaning of our lives. When the writing appeared on the wall of the banqueting hall of the ancient king, and the prophet interpreted it, the supreme charge made against the voluptuous, drunken Belshazzar was, "The God in whose hand thy breath is, and whose are all thy ways, hast thou not glorified." Man's likeness in the deepest fact of his personality is a likeness to God, though the image be marred beyond recognition by any except God Himself. He sees the likeness, and all the possibilities are God-created, whether material, mental, moral or spiritual. Whatever use men may be making of them, they are part of the Divine origin and creation. Let it be said bluntly, the devil never made a blade of grass. He has destroyed much. He never created a capacity. He is always aiming at the destruction of the material, mental, or spiritual. Every power has come from God: the physical which enables us to see, to hear, to touch; the mental, which enables us to think, calculate, and arrange; the spiritual, that haunting inner sense that awakens in every man ever and anon, surprisingly, telling him he is more than flesh, that he is fire.

With that fundamental fact of relationship in mind, we find next the story of separation. What a story it is. The son came to his father and said to him, "Give me the portion of thy substance that falleth to me." The word there means *being,* all the things that make for being. What made him say that to his father? The request was a revelation of the fact that he had lost confidence in his father. There was in his mind an idea that his father stood between him and something that he supremely desired, which he considered would be better for him than the things it was possible for him to have in the father's house and under the father's restraint.

That is the old story according to this Book. That is how sin entered human life in the Garden. The enemy suggested that God was holding something back. "Yea, hath God said?" Well, it is not so. Take that, and you shall be as gods. God is keeping back from you something, a godlike quality which you ought to have. That was the devil's voice, and that is what this young fellow felt. That is the whole tragedy of sin. That is what is the matter with humanity. "Give me the portion of thy substance that falleth to me," and his father gave him what he asked.

Then came the voluntary act. The son decided to act alone. He decided to leave for the far country, and the farther, the better. He would break away from restraint, the law of the father's house, these requirements of his father's house. He went far from home, far from love, far from restraint, and he went away from what he did not recognize at the moment, the guidance that would help him in any crisis.

That is the story of sin. While not denying the fact of our relationship to the race and the fact of racial sin, I would insist that we may so place the emphasis upon that fact of racial sin as to miss the fact of personal wrongdoing and sin. What is the matter with men today? They are away, and have gone as far away from God as they can, even though there may be some who recognize Him with certain gestures, when in all the actualities of their lives they are managing for themselves. So far is that true, I may quote a common saying, which is banal in its commonplaceness and tragic in its revelation. Some man is pointed out to me, apparently a great success in the world, and I am told he is a self-made man. What a stupid lie it is. No man is self-made originally, and no man is self-made, whatever the position he may have made for himself. Many years ago a man came to see me after a service, and said, "I am interested in all you have said, but I do not believe a word of it." When a man talks like that, it is better than anyone who says he believes, when he does not believe at all. This man said, "You tell me I ought to worship God." Then he said this amazing thing: "I have nothing to thank God for." In a moment like that, when we are startled out of our own common sense, one is given something to say. I looked at him, and I said, "Is that so? Are you a strong man?" "Oh, yes," he replied, "I am." I said to him, "How much have you spent on doctor's bills lately?" "Not a penny." "And yet you have nothing to thank God for?" He might have said as many others might say, "My health is due to my own care." Oh, fools and blind. Every breath we draw, we draw in God's air and exhale. If man poisons it, and we get poisoned because man has poisoned it, that is another matter. We cannot live without the ability to breathe. We cannot live without God's water. I can live very well without water man has poisoned, but I cannot live without water. It is God's world, and God's gifts are bestowed upon us. The trouble is we have taken them, and have said we can manage ourselves, and we do not want God.

That is all very well at first. I can almost believe that the journey into the far country was rather a pleasant one. He felt it rather good to be free. Oh, damnably luring and deceptive word oftentimes, but that is what he felt.

[*18*]

In going he had put himself outside home and love, restriction and guidance. That is the story of human sin, of yours and mine. He was a son, but a son who had formed a wrong opinion about his father, and had a false conceit of himself. This is not a lonely story. It is the story of all sin.

Here we leave our first study. Oh, that I had the voice to say to all the little children what was expressed in the words of Longfellow to them.

"Stay, stay at home, my heart, and rest;
 Home-keeping hearts are happiest,
For those who wander they know not where,
 Are full of trouble and full of care;
To stay at home is best.

"Weary and homesick, and distressed;
 They wander east, they wander west,
And are baffled, and beaten, and blown about
 By the winds of the wilderness of doubt;
To stay at home is best.

"Then stay at home, my heart, and rest;
 The bird is safest in its nest;
O'er all that flutter their wings and fly
 A hawk is hovering in the sky;
To stay at home is best."

## The Parable of the Father's Heart

Or if I speak to the youth and the maiden who have gone beyond childhood, Are you in the far country, dear lad, dear maiden? Are you there? How did you come there? Have you prayed recently? Have you worshipped? Are you acknowledging God, and yielding to His holy and beneficent requirements? How did you get into the far country? Somewhere you doubted God, and made a bid for freedom, believing, though perhaps you never formulated a belief in God, that you could manage your life better than God could manage it. Or are you in the far country because father and mother never told you these things? That is the tragedy of all tragedies. There are fathers who feed their children and educate them, and amuse them, and do nothing else; and are surprised when a child breaks away from restraint and brings tragedy, disaster, and ruin upon himself or herself. Did your parents never tell you?

Well, if you are in the far country, go back home before your situation is hopeless. There is no necessity to go as far as this young man did, that you should reach the uttermost depravity before turning back home.

Somewhere there is a man or woman who has spent all, someone who is in want in the land of plenty, someone who has known famine, and no man to give to him. You are in the far country, destitute. What shall I say to you? Go on and finish the story. See what this man did, and do the same. See how the father received the returning son. Though the road be long, the Father is hastening on the way to meet you, and if you have had time to make yourself presentable, the Father's kiss is on your cheek, and His arms are about you. Robe, ring, and sandals await the lost one.

# II

## FEEDING SWINE

*There he wasted his substance with riotous living. And when he had spent all, there arose a mighty famine in that country; and he began to be in want. And he went and joined himself to one of the citizens of that country; and he sent him into his fields to feed swine. And he would fain have been filled with the husks that the swine did eat; and no man gave unto him.*—LUKE xv.13b-16.

THAT is the story of descent to the depths. Happy is the man who discovers his folly soon, and goes back home. For such there need be no fathoming of the depths. I have sometimes thought we preachers have been in danger of preaching as though the Gospel was only for the utterly degraded and depraved. Thank God it is for that man; but there is no need that any one should reach those uttermost depths of degradation. No premium is to be placed on vulgar sin. Happy is the man who early discovers the folly of attempting to govern his own life by taking his substance from God and wasting it

[ 22 ]

in the far country, and then turns his face homeward and receives the welcome of his father.

In these brief and pregnant sentences our Lord has shown the ultimate result of leaving home, of turning one's back on the Father, on God, and going away from His restriction to the far country. It is one of the most marvelous pictures in literature.

Some people are old enough to remember the pictures drawn by William Hogarth called *The Rake's Progress*. In them Hogarth strikingly portrayed a man in surroundings of culture, elegance, and wealth breaking away, and going from bad to worse, until he is at last in the gutter. They were very striking pictures, but as a presentation of the truth as found in our story, they fall far short of Jesus' amazing revelation of what such degradation means. There are multitudes of people in the world today who are not down in the gutter. They have never passed through the material experiences that rob them of everything, and in that sense they are not down. Hogarth's series of pictures would not portray them at all. But these people are in the gutter. They are away from God. They are as desolate as that man whom Hogarth pictured, and our Lord, with that finality of teaching which was always His—for never man spake as

[ *23* ]

He spoke—has given us simple sentences, one succeeding the other, sketching briefly, graphically, forcefully, the downward course, until the ultimate depths are reached.

Leaving out much of the verbiage, read again the sevenfold description in short phrases. "He wasted his substance." "He spent all." "There arose a mighty famine." "He began to be in want." "He was sent to feed swine." "He would fain have been filled with the husks." "No man gave unto him." That is the whole story, and it applies not only to such a one as Hogarth pictured in his remarkable sketches, but to humanity wherever it has turned its back on God and sought for enfranchisement within its own will and government. We will glance at those sentences. It is the story of decline, and yet every stage is an experience, and the whole is full of force and suggestion.

First, when he reached the far country, what did he do? "He wasted his substance with riotous living." That is so simple. If we are not careful we do not grasp the significance of it. What is waste? I think it may be defined simply and sufficiently as disbursement of possessions without adequate return, taking the substance of life and expending it in such a way as to squander it without any abiding satisfaction or proper return. "He wasted his substance with riotous living." There is really a repetition here, for the word *riotous* means without saving. He took the gifts his father bestowed on him, and spent them in the far country, without making provision for leaner days and the ultimate needs of life. Paul uses the same word, in effect, when he said, "Be not drunken with wine, wherein is riot, but be filled with the Spirit." Riotous living is wasteful living, the scattering of forces that bring back no return. That is the first thing we read about this man.

What did he waste? "His substance." He had been to his father and had said, "Give me the portion of thy substance that falleth to me," and his father had given him what he asked. He had come into possession of gifts from his father. So man is seen here going out from God to waste his substance, *God's* substance. The root idea of the word *substance* is that of being, all the forces from God that make life. All the forces that are being expended today in iniquity and wickedness are Divine forces prostituted, squandered. Man has nothing in that sense that he has not received from God. At the back of the loaf the snowy flour, the mill, and the miller, and the farmer; and at the back of the farmer, God. "Give us this day our daily bread," and we cannot get it save from God. All man's resources are Divine gifts. I have been in this world over threescore years. During those years I have been breathing its air, eating its food provided for me. All my material life, all the powers with which God has so wondrously blessed me through the years, they are His. What have I done with them? They are gone beyond recall. I cannot call back a single ounce of energy I have expended. What have I done with them? I am only asking the question.

Or pass from the physical to the mental, the powers of thought, observation, comparison, deduction—all the wonderful mental activities of a human life. These have been spent for what, and with what result?

Or rise to a higher level, and think of moral considerations, the admiration of goodness and the hatred of evil which are common to all humanity, however depraved. There is no roué in our great city who does not know in his deepest heart the beauty of goodness. What has been done with these moral conceptions?

Or, finally, those spirtual forces that ever and anon bring us vision, and a sense of the larger, the vaster, the eternal—what have we done with them? What are the returns from this expenditure of substance?

That is the test question for every life. Have we anything resulting from our expenditure of these forces, of which we can say, This is the result, and this will abide, whatever else may perish? There was satire in the word of the old Hebrew prophet, addressed to the people of God, "Ye have sold yourselves for naught." A man may say, I have done very well, I have made my fortune. What is your fortune? What has it gotten for you? What do you possess? Do you possess it? Oh, no, you do not possess it. A few short years at the very most and your hand will not sign checks, you will be a dead hand on future generations, and men will fling it off sooner or later. We go on living, spending our powers, material, mental, moral and spiritual; and when we take stock there is no balance, there is nothing left, nothing we can hold, nothing of which we can say, It is ours. Remember what Jesus said to His own disciples, "Lay not up for yourselves treasures upon the earth, where moth and rust doth consume, and where thieves break through and steal; but lay up for yourselves treasures in heaven." Have we any treasure laid up there? A man who has turned his back upon God has none. He is bounded by the present. His gold has brought him no return, so far as his output of energy is concerned. He has wasted his substance.

Mark how it is immediately followed by the second phase. "When he had spent all." That is the inevitable issue of waste. The hour of utter extremity arrives when the capital is all gone, and when a man has no argosies on the seas which presently will be returning, bringing him the returns for his expenditure. "When he had spent all." Waste will bring every man there sooner or later in some form. I need not stress the physical. No one can take physical forces and abuse them and waste them and scatter them without weakening them. Our hospitals are full of such cases. No one can take mental powers and misuse them without ruining them until they cease to act. Our mental asylums are full proof of that. Moral powers cannot be denied. The moral consciousness which forgets the perpetual necessity for reconstruction and renewal of fellowship with God presently becomes dead. There are some terrible expressions in the New Testament, "a dead conscience," "a conscience seared as with a hot iron," that is, a conscience that has lost its sensitiveness. When this man began his life by voluntary separation from God, and went to the far country, there went with him a moral consciousness that made him blush when he told a lie, that made him feel awkward when he heard or told a story that brushed the bloom of modesty from the cheek of youth; but he has lost the power to blush, and is impure without sense of awkwardness today. He is a wreck. He has spent all.

Immediately we pass to the next phrase. "There arose a mighty famine in that land." I do not believe that Jesus meant that when he had spent all there came a famine that had not existed before, but that to the man who had spent all there arose a mighty famine. There is famine everywhere when men have spent all, physically and materially. London or any city is the home of famine to the man who has nothing. If a man has spent his all physically the city of plenty is the city of famine and of destitution. There is nothing in the far country when a man has run through Divinely bestowed gifts. The far country has no currency of its own. A man can get out of it only what he puts into it. A man may say, I am getting a great deal out of the far country, laughter and merriment. I am having what the world calls a good time. I am seeing life. All the things you are getting out you are putting in, the things with which God has endowed you. Spend them apart from His control and presently, in the midst of laughter, you will be in agony; in the midst of plenty you will be dying of hunger. There was a mighty famine when he had spent all. As long as he had anything to spend there was no famine; but oh, my masters, when material strength has gone, mental forces are wasted, the moral sense is dead, and the spiritual vision ended; then famine follows. "There arose a mighty famine in that country."

"And he began to be in want." Although we are tracing the story of this man's descent to the depths I see here the first gleam of hope, but this man is by no means at the end of the darkness. "He began to be in want." The first sense of the distance of the far country broke upon him. When a man begins to be in want he will try, for all he is worth, to deny his want. Sometimes he will try to cover it with flippancy, sometimes with cynicism, sometimes with professed agnosticism. Behind much of the flippancy of some people, and the cynicism of others, and agnosticism with all its flaunting imperiousness there lies the hunger of the soul which the man is trying to cover up, and refuses to acknowledge.

That sense often makes a man take refuge in prolonged rebellion. That is seen here in this story. When this man began to be in want he went and joined himself to a citizen of the far country. Why did he not go home? Men do not do that. They prolong their return. They will not go back at once. This man had hardly begun to think seriously about the things he had left at home, so he joined himself to a citizen of the far country into which he had gone.

The next word is that the citizen "sent him into his fields to feed swine." We can only get the full impact of this statement in the light of the outlook of the country in which the words were spoken, and in the light of the fact that Jesus was addressing Himself to Hebrews, to the rulers, the Pharisees and scribes. He used an expression that to them meant the uttermost degradation. This man was not going home. He joined himself to a citizen, and what will the citizen do? Send him into his fields to feed swine. He prolonged his degradation; indeed, he deepened his degradation. That was the estimate of the citizen of the far country of this man's worth. Go and feed my swine. The whole picture becomes powerfully graphic.

We can translate it into the language of today, and into some experiences we have seen and watched. There is a public-house loafer yonder. He is an Oxford graduate, but there is nothing he does but hang around for a pint of beer and a chuck-out! One of the most appalling and tragic experiences of my life was the memory of a preacher of marvelous power, under whose spell men sat with wonder and amazement; and the last thing I know of that man was that in a public-house he was preaching an old sermon for the amusement of the crowd, and the payment of half a pint of beer. You say, my friend, young man, I am never coming to that. How do you know? Do you suppose he ever meant to come to that? In an evil hour he took his substance, and began to forget the government of God, and wandered until he had spent all, and then the citizen of the far country sent him to feed swine. That is the abiding application of the story.

Then what? "He began to be in want." Not only did he begin to be in want, but "he would fain have been filled with the husks that the swine did eat." Here we are face to face with the tragedy of the spiritual, the hunger of soul. Let us quickly add the last sentence of all, "No man gave unto him." That is the story. Their only interest in him was that as a machine for feeding their pigs. Each for himself! If he fails, let him die. That is all the far country has for any man. He has spent his substance, and is in want. The deepest hunger of his life is asserting itself. The far country has nothing to give. "No man gave unto him." Why not? Because in this realm of the material the law of the survival of the fittest is the only law. Spend the forces of life without reference to God in the midst of riotous companionships, in ways of wickedness, gaining no return, having no reserve, and presently, when all is gone, famine will come, and hunger is there. The far country will give nothing, will have no pity, no sympathy, no help. Shall I surprise you when I say that the law of the survival of the fittest is an excellent one. It is one that obtains through all life. Why should failure be perpetuated? Is it not wholly beneficent that the world will have no wastrels?

But that is not the story in its finality. There is Someone who will give, if no man gave unto him. The only basis on which God saves a man is that he shall be remade. While the world's method of flinging out the man who has wasted his substance is wholly beneficent, we thank God for the evangel. Take the Gospel away, and there is no hope for such a man, because the world cannot feed him, or reconstruct him, or remake him. It has no philosophy that is equal to it, no force that can accomplish it; and therefore the best thing it can do is to let him die lest he spoil other lives.

Thank God there is One who came to seek and save the lost. Over against this wholly beneficent and Divine principle of the survival of the fittest, we have the great message of salvation, the remaking of the individual. Let the law of the survival of the fittest work itself out in heartlessness and brutality as it seems, until the man be flung on to the world's scrap heap; then, thank God, there is One who comes and puts His hand on that scrap heap, takes hold of the rubbish, and makes it again. That is the Gospel. He can make the desert blossom as the rose. He can take the wrecked, ruined, burnt-out and spoiled life and remake it, and ere His work is done, He will present it faultless before the throne of God. He is watching over the sinner, waiting for his home-coming, running already on the rough road to meet him, to place on his cheek the kiss of eternal pardon.

# III

## RETURNING REASON

*But when he came to himself he said, How many hired servants of my father's have bread enough and to spare, and I perish here with hunger! I will arise and go to my father, and will say unto him, Father, I have sinned against heaven, and in thy sight; I am no more worthy to be called thy son; make me as one of thy hired servants.—LUKE xv.17-19.*

WE HAVE followed this man to the far country, and have seen him pass to the depths. We have seen in him a revelation of humanity in its definite break with God. He left his father. He attempted to escape from the restrictions of his father's house. He went out feeling that he could manage his own affairs better than his father could; and he traveled away—significant phrase—to the "far country," a long way off, for his purposes, the farther the better.

We have seen him descending to the depths through those processes which, in simple and yet sublime and searching sentences, our Lord employed. We saw him wasting his substance with riotous living. We saw him conscious of famine that arose in the land. We saw him brought to the place of absolute penury. Then we saw him still persisting in an independent attitude, joining himself to a citizen of the far country. We have seen the estimate that citizen had of him. The citizen sent him into his fields to feed swine. So we have followed him from home to the far country, and have seen him going to the depths.

This study opens with a very significant word: "When he came to himself." Standing at the center of the story, these words reveal the true meaning of this man's former action, and indicate the way by which he returned. To use the figure, it is a light in the midst of the passage, flashing both ways, illuminating all that we have seen, and revealing so far as this man was concerned, the meaning of all now to be considered.

"When he came to himself." That opens the way to home and restoration. "He came to himself." What does that mean? We can state the whole fact at the beginning in a few sentences. In all the processes in which we saw him going to the far country, and descending to the depths, he was mad, he was beside himself; his actions were characterized by insanity. "But when he came to himself," the contrast is seen immediately. What a change is here, a change in outlook, a change in purpose. All the things that followed that dawn of reason proved that his action from that moment was the action of sanity.

Here, then, we have a revelation of the insanity of godlessness, and the sanity of godliness. The outsider, the man of the world, often looks on those living a godly life as being a little short in some ways. When Festus said to Paul, "Paul, thou art mad; thy much learning doth turn thee to madness," he heard Paul speak of his life and faith and Gospel. The cynical man of the world said he was mad, and that idea still obtains. Perhaps in these days it does not express itself in that way, but there are many people, our friends in the social set, who really think there is something queer about us, that religion is characterized by a certain form of insanity. But the true rationalist—to redeem this word from a possible abuse—is the believer, the Christian man, who is living his life in right relationship with God, willingly, submissively. That is the life of reason as well as the life of faith. This man here went down, until he was in the depths; and suddenly reason dawned, and then "he came to himself."

## The Parable of the Father's Heart

In the simplest way, take that conception and watch this man in the light of it, and in the light of the man's story look at human life when lived apart from the Father's home and government, in other words, apart from God. All the signs which we associate with insanity on the ordinary plane of life are to be found in the action of this man.

One of the first evidences of insanity is loss of memory. One sign of insanity is that things are forgotten. I need not stay to argue that. In the early days of his sojourn in the far country this man lived his life without thought of his father and his home, and of his relationship to both. That may be a piece of mere speculative interpretation. Then treat the story on its simplest human level, not as a story of nineteen centuries ago, but as a story of a young man in similar conditions today, one who gathers from his father his share of property, takes his way to another land and spends it. The most surprising thing is that man's forgetfulness of his relationship to his father, and his responsibility to his father. It was Carlyle who once declared that the being the devil dreaded the most is the man who dares to think. It is a perfectly true statement. Yet this loss of memory, this life lived in forgetfulness of essential relationships and abiding truths is the first evidence of insanity.

When they charged Hamlet with being mad, he said,

"Bring me to the test,
And I the matter will reward, which madness
Would gambol from."

In other words, he said, I have not lost my memory; bring me to the test. Here is a Biblical description of the godless life. "All his thoughts are, There is no God." There is a fine, subtle irony in that word. The thoughts of the godless man are characterized by forgetfulness of God, through all his life, in his thinking, planning, arranging. Jesus drew another picture of this life in another parable, that of the rich fool, the man who lived in the midst of fertile fields, and in prosperity, and thought only of his fruits, his barns, his corn, his goods; until, like a crack of thunder, came the arresting word, "But God said unto him, Thou foolish one, this night is thy soul required of thee." Are we living there? The recitation of the creed on Sunday is no proof that God is remembered; nor is joining in the worship of the sanctuary, if God is referred to in a restless hour of irksome worship on the Sabbath. If He be forgotten on six days, it is the first alarming evidence of spiritual insanity, and the wearisome and empty performance on the seventh is of no value.

But another evidence of madness is that of having distorted views, so that certain persons are mistaken for others. In that masterly delineation of madness in Shakespeare's *King Lear,* the king could not tell the difference between Edgar and the fool, and attributed to the fool all wisdom, and to Edgar all folly. Nothing is sadder than to go through the mournful wards or corridors of an insane asylum and see those who have lost their reason imagining that they are someone else, not understanding things, and having a false view altogether. There was a man who on one occasion said he was Julius Cæsar, and at another time he changed his mind, and declared he was Napoleon Bonaparte. Distorted views. This man taking his journey to the far country, the thought of his heart was expressed in the action of his life. In his heart he thought of his father as being hard and unkind, and of those men he would meet in the far country as being generous and kind. These were distorted views indeed. He was ignorant of himself and of his father. He was mad.

Take another note of madness here, his inability to appreciate relative values. I look at the things he gives, and examine what he gets, and I see at once this man has lost his sense of relative values. Everything must be tested by that standard in the matter of bartering. If I see children playing by the roadside, exchanging in their play beads for beads, beads of glass, crystal, green, red, blue, that is fine. But if I saw them bartering beads for jewels, diamonds, sapphires, emeralds, and rubies, I should say there was something wrong here; it is a sign of insanity, though the children might not have known what they were doing. One sign of insanity is that we do not know relative values. Here this man is seen turning his back on home and love and compassion for the companions of the far country, choosing "the pleasures of sin for a season" rather than the pleasures which are the gift of God. To do this is to put out of the life all wealth and richness of God's purpose, and to take, instead, all the beggarly emptiness and poverty of the world.

Again, I find in this man's action loss of business acumen. That, every business man will admit, is a sure evidence of insanity. The man who takes his capital and lives on it without investing it, how does he end? There is one short and brutal answer, which tells all the truth—in bankruptcy! That is the story here. He received substance from his father. He spent it. He did not invest it. That is the ultimate proof of insanity.

Yet look once again. We have seen his loss of memory, and forgetfulness of his father. What did this really mean? The death of love. If he had not lost the power of love he never would have wounded the heart of his father as he did. Love was stifled, killed, trampled on, until it was nonexistent.

And yet once more: pride, self-satisfaction, the ignorance of madness. This man did not know how mad he was. Is there any madness worse than the madness of such pride, and the unconsciousness of it all? That magnificent independence in which he made his boast is unutterable madness. He was masquerading in the robes of royalty, but was unable to administer the affairs of the kingdom. Can there be anything more mad than that?

So, finally, self-destruction, not necessarily immediate. At the back of all his action was lack of recognition of the first law of human life, the law of self-preservation. The surest suicide is the persistent sinner who goes on in his godlessness. Many men commit suicide over whom no coroner pronounces such a verdict. Life is wasted, flung away, expended, issuing in self-destruction.

"But when he came to himself." Everything is at once changed, and as we watch, all that follows stands in striking contrast to those notes of madness which we have seen.

"He came to himself," and at once memory reasserted itself. He thought of the old days and the old conditions that he felt were still obtaining there. He thought of that which he had endeavored to forget. He began to think. My father's house, my father's hired servants, they are not hungry. They are not destitute. There is bread there to spare. These things are becoming real to him again.

His madness had been characterized by distorted views. With the return of the true balance of reason he comes to right views. Notice how he said again and again, "my father." There is always a threnody in it. There he was in his loneliness and desolation, but he had come to himself, and was naming his father as he ought to be named. That is another sign of returning reason when the soul begins to recognize its relation to God and that "God is love."

In his madness we saw that he had no appreciation of relative values. Listen to him as he balanced accounts. It is better to serve at

[ *43* ]

home than to reign here. Freedom here has become slavery. Service there was freedom. I pause here, because it is something many do not believe even today. One of the profoundest words revealing the essence of sin is found in Milton's *Paradise Lost,* words put into the lips of Lucifer, son of the morning, whom Milton describes as falling from his high estate. They reveal the inwardness of Satan's fall,

"To reign is worth ambition, though in hell;
  Better to reign in hell, than serve in heaven."

It was a daring thing for Milton to put such a sentiment into Lucifer's lips, and yet how accurate and true it is. Yet that is the supreme evidence that the devil is the ultimate lunatic of the universe, because he does not reign in hell. God reigns in hell. The devil cannot touch a single hair on the back of a single camel that belongs to Job until he has Divine permission, nor can he sift the disciples as wheat. He may think he reigns, but God reigns.

If we take that from the immediate application of the fall of Lucifer and apply it to a man it becomes true. No man reigns. He thinks he does. That is his madness, and the return of reason is seen when he comes to the decision that he was wrong, that it would be better to go home and become a hired servant than to live in the far country as he has come to live, and suffer as he has suffered.

Mark also the return of mental acumen. He had taken his capital and spent it, without investing it. He will now go back, not to invest any capital, for he has none to invest, but to invest his own strength, whatever may be left of it, in the service of his father. "Make me as one of thy hired servants." Take my life, and let me serve. It is the return to reason.

Love was coming back. Memory of his father was coming, and humility had come. He was going back to say to his father, "I have sinned." That is one of the most difficult sentences human lips can ever utter. It is quite easy to say we are all sinners. It is a very different thing to say, I have sinned. It is so in human relationships. There is many a home that never would have been broken up if a man, or a woman, had dared to say, I have sinned. That is the language of humility. It is the language of shame. It is the courage of penitence. "I have sinned," I am not worthy. Make me a servant. When reason takes possession of the soul again, a man says immediately, I have sinned. Humility is the evidence of the dawn of reason.

Finally, in going away to the far country

there was forgetfulness of the first law of life, that of self-preservation. Listen to him. "I perish with hunger! I will arise, and go to my father." In that decision there is evidence of the return of reason, for he denies himself in order to find himself.

The godless life is the life of madness, insanity. The fashion of the godless world is to think and speak of godly men as those who are lacking in reason. It is the godly life that is rational, the life of sanity. All this is dependent on the foundation fact of man's peculiar relation to God by first creation. This man was a son. He had relationship with God. To deny that, and have some other view of man—there is no meaning in all this. If man is only an animal, and has sprung from animal beginnings, and has moved up, then I think he has done remarkably well. Only, my masters, there are signs of reversion to type! The world is full of evidences that man is going back to the slime, to the jungle, to beastliness. This is only an aside, so banish it. We do not believe that of man. We believe in his fall from his high estate, that he was made in the image and likeness of God, and it is that conception that lies at the back of this parable.

Have we come to ourselves? We have all

been taking our substance and spending it. I do not say we are wasting it. It is gone. What have we to show? Are you conscious of bankruptcy in the spiritual realm, bankruptcy of the fine dignity of personality according to the Divine ideal? Have you come to yourself? Are you beginning to understand that? Stripped of all accidentals, where are you? Are you awaking? Then I tell you, what you need is home, and to get home.

"What is the cry of a child
  Lost in endless streets, or in stubbled fields forgotten,
  Even 'mid forest joys or by ocean's changing wonders?
  Surely he cries, his piteous infant accents broken,
   'I want to go home!'

"What is the cry of a man
  Spent with painful toil or wiith pleasure's vain endeavour,
  Maimed with rude buffets dealt by Time's encroaching fingers?
  Surely he cries, his quivering tones age-worn and weary,
   'I want to go home!'

"What is the cry of a soul
  Wandering forlorn through straining hosts, unhailed, unheeded,

## The Parable of the Father's Heart

Lost in a mist of anguish, seeing afar the glory?
Surely it cries, whether young or old, with a bitter
  wailing
  'I want to go home!' "

Is anyone saying that? Then there is the
remainder of the parable. Start the journey
home. Tramp, however hard the way, and ere
long you will find the open door, and the Father
greeting you. Go home!

# IV

## THE WELCOME HOME

*And he arose, and came to his father. But while he
was yet afar off, his father saw him, and was moved
with compassion, and ran, and fell on his neck, and
kissed him. And the son said unto him, Father, I
have sinned against heaven, and in thy sight: I am
no more worthy to be called thy son. But the father
said to his servants, Bring forth quickly the best robe,
and put it on him; and put a ring on his hand, and
shoes on his feet: and bring the fatted calf, and kill
it, and let us eat, and make merry; for this my son
was dead, and is alive again; he was lost, and is
found. And they began to be merry.—LUKE xv.20-24.*

WE NOW reach the true value of this familiar story. The events we have previ-
ously considered have been of value, but, after
all, they have been incidental and preparatory.
This has been an unveiling of the departure of
humanity from God, and God's attitude toward
humanity, as pictured in the rebellious and returning son.

As a story it is natural, simple, human. It

[ *49* ]

is not at all difficult to believe that when Jesus
uttered these words He had some actual father
in His mind, some actual son in His thought.
We have seen the whole procedure repeated constantly in our own observation. The essential
humanity of it appeals to the heart. The finest
instincts of men recognize the beauty of the
story. That has made it so popular. Everyone
knows the story, and no one quarrels with any
part of it, until we come to the elder son. Thus
the story is in keeping with the whole process of
Incarnation, wherein Christ came to reveal God
to man through men. Jesus takes a human picture to show us God. He is able to do this because man is the offspring of God.

In these verses there are four things to
notice. First, the welcome which the returning
son received. Secondly, the interrupted prayer
which the son offered. Third, the reinstatement
which the father made. Finally, we shall take
one brief glance at the picture of the home life
with which the story ends.

Look first at his welcome. We can add
nothing to the actual words, but consider these
great sentences. "While he was yet afar off his
father saw him." The son had gone to the far
country. He was coming back from that far
country; but while he was still afar off his father

saw him. Take the human story. May we not be sure that his father had been watching for him, had never forgotten him, had never given him up? How often the eyes of the old man had rested on that highway, or had looked toward the distant hills; and now, at last, he saw his son coming, saw him afar off, and knew him. He was changed, probably he was literally in rags, possibly unkempt, haggard. I wonder if anyone else would have recognized him so far off, anyone except his father.

That is the first thing to be noticed. The lesson is that God is ever watching and waiting for the home-coming of those who are in rebellion against Him, have taken their substance and wandered away, and wasted it in riotous living. God is always watching, waiting for their home-coming, and no scars of sin can efface the image of God from the eyes of God. Oh, yes, the scars of sin can efface the image of God from the eyes of men. We have seen human faces in which it would be very difficult to trace any likeness to the Divine image. We could not see it, but God could see it. He sees beneath all the disfigurement, all the bruising, the marring, the battering, the Divine likeness. When the boy was far off, when the father first saw him, almost unrecognizable, the father knew him.

## The Parable of the Father's Heart

There comes back to me an illustration, the story of a Scotch lassie who broke away from home and restraint. She went to the far country, and fell into sin, terrible sin, and went down to the depths, until she was derelict. And, like this boy, she had nothing left. Ruined in every way, she traced her way back home, and arrived at her mother's cottage in the night. When she came up the winding lane that led to the cottage she was amazed to see a light shining in the window in the middle of the night. She trembled, and feared that her mother was ill. She quickened her footsteps, noticed that the door of the cottage was open, and then paused. Her mother heard her footsteps, and knew them, and swiftly she ran down the stairs to her lassie. "Mother, what is the matter? Why is the door open? What is the light burning for?" "Janie, that light has never been out a night nor the door shut since you went away!" Motherhood, Fatherhood, God! "His father saw him," the father knew him.

Go on to the next sentence. I cannot add anything to this. He "was moved with compassion." At this point in the story I am always inclined to be critical, looking at it as a human story merely. When this old man saw his son, he started running to meet him. Such action seems

at first to be characterized by an utter absence
of dignity. "He ran." Yet look again! Absence
of dignity? I tell you it was the demonstration of
complete dignity because it was inspired by compassion. He was moved with pity, and he ran.
As the prophet said, "A God ready to pardon."
All the superficialities of false dignity are sub-
merged and swept aside, and in the dignity of
a great love he ran to meet his boy.

Let us reverently climb from the illustration, as Christ intended that we should. This
is Christ's picture of God. I dare not have drawn
such a picture, or made such a suggestion. I believe in a God holy, high, eternal, who occupies
the throne from everlasting to everlasting. These
human eyes have been so accustomed to associate
with that throne an authority and a dignity
which bends with difficulty. But He who shares
that throne has drawn the picture, and says, If
you would know, son of God wandering in the
far country, wasting your substance, remembering God with breaking heart, how you will be
received if you return to Him, then this is the
picture. God runs to meet you with an eagerness
born of His compassion.

What next? The father fell on the son's
neck, and smothered him with kisses. That is it.
He kissed him very much. Hold on! I am in-

clined to stand back, and to be critical. I look at the picture and say, Is not that a sign of weakness? Dismiss the thought. It was a sign of strength. Would it not have been better to wait until the boy had made acknowledgment of his wrongdoing? No, the father knew his boy. He knew that the boy would make his confession best when his head was pillowed on his father's breast. He did not wait for him to be clothed. He did not wait for him to be cleansed. He put his arms round the boy's neck, smothered him with kisses that marked reconciliation and pardon, tokens that in the father's heart he was reinstated immediately, seeing he had set his face towards home, and had tramped the long distance, and had arrived there.

That is a wonderful picture of the sure impression of the love of God made on the spirit of man when he comes back to God. Perhaps those who have been farthest away understand it best. They come back to find a forgiveness that also forgets. Do not miss that. We may say, Can God forget anything? Yes, in this sense, "Thy sins and thine iniquities will I remember against thee no more for ever." Yes, a forgiveness in that sense forgets. That is so different from us. Somebody says, I have forgiven that man, but I shall never forget his wrongdoing. That is why we are so unlike God. Such a man who says that must be related to the elder son! God forgives, and God forgets.

Now listen to the interrupted prayer. To understand it we must go back and read again the previous verses. He had said to himself in the far country, "I will arise and go to my father, and will say unto him, Father, I have sinned against heaven, and in thy sight; I am no more worthy to be called thy son; make me as one of thy hired servants." That is the prayer. But notice he never got through it. Listen to him, "I have sinned against heaven and in thy sight; I am no more worthy to be called thy son": and at that point the father broke in on the prayer, interrupted it, ended it. He intended to say, I have sinned, I have forfeited my rights; let my degradation continue. I do not ask to be reinstated as a son. Let me atone for what I have done by what I will do. Let me serve. Let me wipe out the sin and shame of the years in which I have wasted substance, wounded thy heart, by going without sandals, by being a slave in thy household. I have learned that it is better to serve at home than to reign in the far country. But he had no time to finish. He never got the chance to say, Make me as one of thy hired servants. He had said enough. He had said the thing necessary to say—"I have sinned," or to take the Greek word and put it into common language, "I have missed the mark." What I thought was right was wrong. What I thought was liberty was slavery. It was necessary that he should say, "I have sinned, I am no more worthy to be called thy son." Past sin leaves its effect. I have forfeited all my right. Pride was humbled, shame was experienced, and confession was made. But he never got any further.

This was not impertinent repentance, saying, I have made my acknowledgment, and now it is your business to reinstate me. He was permitted to say another thing, "I am no more worthy to be called thy son." This man took his position on his father's breast, not because he dared to seek that position, but because grace had placed him there in infinite love. His degradation was not in the will of his father. It was not the father's will that he had gone away, and now he would not perpetuate the boy's wrongdoing. Menial service will not atone. The service of tomorrow will never atone for the sin of yesterday.

This is where so many people make a mistake. At the beginning of the year we make good resolutions. I am not against such resolutions. Someone has said the way to hell is paved with good intentions. But so is the way to heaven. Resolutions may be quite good. We say we are going to turn over a new leaf. What a curious figure of speech that is. What do we mean? We mean that we have sinned, we have blotted the page, and have smirched the escutcheon. Here is the record up to now, and it is blotted as badly as can be. We turn over a new leaf. What is to be done with those leaves we have turned over? We cannot undo them. We cannot blot them out. When that new leaf is turned over, nothing can be done to right the wrong done, and to right the record of the past pages of the years. It is no use turning over a new leaf in that way. The probability is we shall do as badly on the new one as on the old. No, don't turn over a new leaf. Take a new book from the pierced Hand, put your hand in His, and as my mother held my hand when she taught me to write, let Him hold your hand as you write the story. We cannot by service undo anything of the past. The Father does not ask it. He will break in on your prayer.

But there is no need. What will the father say? "Bring forth quickly the best robe, and put it on him, and put a ring on his hand and shoes on his feet." The prayer was interrupted because there was infinite provision made for the reception of the son through the compassion of the father's heart. Not by what he is able to do can the son atone, but by that which is done for him, apart from him. By that which is made over to him in infinite grace, so is atonement made.

Do not forget that this part of the parable is not complete in itself. That we saw in our first study. The three parts of the parable reveal the truth, or rather, three phases of the parable. The first is that of the shepherd, the second that of the woman who seeks. All the method by which grace operates is not revealed in this single aspect of the parable; but the fact is made perfectly clear that provision for the reception of the son is made, not by the son, but by the father, and that it is bestowed on the son out of the exceeding grace of the father's heart.

Finally, let us take a brief glance at that provision. Here again we get back to simplicities which are symbols of sublimities. Put the best robe on him, and a ring on his finger and shoes on his feet. Robe, ring, and royal sandals await the lost one. These three things answer exactly the prayer which he meant to have prayed. The robe is the answer to "I have sinned." The ring is the answer to "I am no more worthy to be called thy son." The sandals constitute the answer to "make me one of thy hired servants." These symbols are Eastern. Put the robe on him, the robe that befits the father's house. Perhaps it is necessary to stay here to notice that the best robe was not put on over the rags, the filthy garments. Some would speak as though the robe of righteousness was put over the sinner's rags to hide them. God is not unclean! There is no doubt a cleansing preceded the robing in the case of this son.

The ring was the sign of relationship, of sonship. "Put a ring on his finger." He is my son. Give him the sign of sonship. By that token give him authority to become a son. So there is not only atonement, but regeneration and re-instatement by that infinite miracle. Put a ring on his finger; bring him back into the relationship that he had forfeited and lost by his sin.

What else? Put shoes on his feet. Still the picture is Eastern. The slave was never permitted to wear shoes. The badge of slavery was the absence of sandals. When Paul was writing of the equipment of the Christian, he said, "Your feet shod with the preparation of the gospel of peace," that is, equipment for service, not the service of a slave, but of a son. Robe, ring, and royal sandals await the lost one.

One final glance at the home. While not

desiring to be controversial, there are some who tell us if we introduce atonement and sacrifice into this story it will have to be rewritten, for that does not appear here. The first answer to that objection is that if so, the whole of the New Testament will have to be rewritten. The second answer is that this story is only one-third of the parable. The parable is a threefold one. It opens wtih the story of the shepherd, and

"None of the ransomed ever knew
  How deep were the waters crossed;
 Nor how dark was the night that the Lord passed
    through
  Ere He found His sheep that was lost."

That is the part of the parable of God, in His Son, ransoming the sinner.

Yet I am not sure that we are correct in saying there is nothing about sacrifice here. The late Professor Samuel Ives Curtiss wrote a valuable book on Semitic religions, the outcome of his personal investigation in the Holy Land of the manners and customs of the people. In the course of it he described how when a young man had been away from home in a distant land, whether as a prodigal or a traveler, on his return it was the custom to offer on the threshold a sacrifice, which sacrifice became the feast of welcome. That is exactly what you find here. In conversation with Dr. Curtiss, I asked him if he had ever applied that custom to the parable of the prodigal son. He said he had never thought of that relationship, but admitted that it was a most interesting thought. This makes it the more valuable. Before this son could get back into his home, sacrifice was necessary in case there had been sin. "Bring forth the fatted calf and kill it, and let us eat." This was the very language which would be understood by all Semitic people.

Do not miss that word *merry*. There was a meal, and merriment, merriment in the home, not that of the far country. There "the pleasures of sin for a season," but now merriment, gladness, assuredly, and dancing. "Let us be merry." Why? My son, as to himself, was dead; now he is alive. As to my own heart, as though the father had said, he was lost, but now he is found.

Yes, there is that dark background of the elder son. He is never called the elder brother in the parable. Of course, he was a brother, but the word is applied to the younger son, and not to the elder. What did he hear? Music and dancing, actual, positive, glorious merriment. We are going to leave him severely alone. It should be remembered that our Lord was talking to a little group of scribes and Pharisees, who had criticized Him when they said, "This man receiveth sinners, and eateth with them." They know so much about God, but they did not know God. So we dismiss him, and you also, if you are related to him.

There is only one question for us to ask. Thank God for all who have come home, who have received the robe and ring and sandals. Is there anyone in the far country, or tramping the way home, half wistfully wondering what is going to happen, and who is prepared to make amends by service? Take this story, and remember He knows; He has seen you; He is running to meet you. May there be a meeting between the returning wanderer and God now.

# V

## A Sequel

*And he spake unto them this parable, saying, What
man of you, having a hundred sheep, and having
lost one of them, doth not leave the ninety and nine
in the wilderness, and go after that which is lost, until he find it? And when he hath found it, he layeth
it on his shoulders, rejoicing. And when he cometh
home, he calleth together his friends and his neighbours, saying unto them, Rejoice with me, for I have
found my sheep which was lost. I say unto you, that
even so there shall be joy in heaven over one sinner
that repenteth, more than over ninety and nine right-
eous persons, who need no repentance.*

*Or what woman having ten pieces of silver, if she
lose one piece, doth not light a lamp, and sweep the
house, and seek diligently until she find it? And
when she hath found it, she calleth together her
friends and neighbours, saying, Rejoice with me, for
I have found the piece which I had lost. Even so, I
say unto you, there is joy in the presence of the angels
of God over one sinner that repenteth.*—LUKE xv.3-10.

THIS study is complementary to the four
previous ones on the prodigal son. The first
ten verses of the chapter contain the first two

[ *63* ]

phases of the one answer of Jesus to the criticism of the scribes and Pharisees.

To understand these two phases it is necessary to go back into the previous chapter in which Luke has told the story of the presence of our Lord in the house of one of the rulers of the Pharisees. There His words had been characterized by almost unusual severity. Then turning from the place where He had been a guest, He spoke some of the sternest words that ever passed His lips concerning the terms of discipleship, and explained the reason of the severity of His terms by the figure of the building of a tower, and the conduct of a warfare, ending all by this most searching word, spoken to all men contemplating following Him, and making Him Lord: "Salt therefore is good; but even if the salt have lost its savour, wherewith shall it be seasoned? It is fit neither for the land nor for the dunghill; men cast it out." Savorless salt men cast out!

We notice the close connection between the last words of that severe discourse, in which He demanded new attention to all that He had been saying, with the affirmation of the first verse of the next chapter: "He that hath ears to hear, let him hear. Now all the publicans and sinners were drawing near unto him, for to hear him." There is striking relationship between these two verses. In spite of the severity of His terms, the publicans and sinners drew near to hear Him. The men most conscious of sin were those most eager to listen to the Voice of unqualified holiness. But there were other men standing around, the scribes and Pharisees, who murmured and complained, and they did so in these words: "This man receiveth sinners, and eateth with them."

Let us at once admit that had He been such as they were, the philosophy underlying their criticism was perfectly correct, and the criticism justified. They meant to say, If this man makes Himself the familiar friend of sinning men, He will Himself become a sinner. As they saw Him receiving into familiar friendship men notoriously sinful, they believed what some of us were taught when we were children, that you cannot touch pitch without being defiled. Show me your friends, and I will foretell your future.

Our Lord answered their philosophy by giving them a revelation of His personality and an explanation of His purpose in the one parable in three, the parable of lost things.

To read this parable aright we must bear in mind that it was spoken in answer to criticism, and that by it He rebuked these men for a false outlook on sinning men and for attempting to compress Him within the narrow compass of their own philosophy. By an unveiling of Himself, and a revelation of the real meaning of His mission in the world, He gave the explanation of why He received sinning men, which caused astonishment and a stumbling-block to the scribes and Pharisees. As I watch the process of that unveiling, I see that He rebuked them, not principally for their failure to understand Him, but for their failure to understand the value of sinning men to the heart of God. In this parable we have His reply to that criticism. They said, "This man receiveth sinners, and eateth with them." He replied, "What man of *you,* having a hundred sheep, and having lost one of them, doth not leave the ninety and nine in the wilderness, and go after that which is lost until he find it?" His meaning is self-evident. You criticize me for sitting and eating with sinners. I do it because they are lost sheep, and I am seeking them.

Then when He came to the second phase of the story He introduced a new tone, thought, and emphasis, those of the motherly element. He went straight on. There is no break between the two phases, that of the lost sheep, and the woman sweeping and searching and finding, and the father. In the third phase of the parable there seems not to be the same pertinent application to the criticism of the Pharisees; but we find at the conclusion that the elder son becomes the picture of their attitude. It is important that we should see the sweep of the study before examining some of the details.

There they stood round about Him, the throng of publicans and sinners, smirched men, soiled women. There He stood in the midst of them, talking to them quite familiarly, in all the expressiveness of the Greek word, receiving them unto Himself, into close, familiar comradeship, sitting down to eat with them, violating all Pharisaic traditions, even without washing His hands. Again, there stand the scribes and Pharisees, the interpreters of the moral law, the teachers of purity, holiness, and righteousness, shocked at His familiarity with sinning men, saying, "This man receiveth sinners, and eateth with them."

Out of the midst of His comradeship with sinners He explains and defends His action. He does what He so often did, makes them the judges. Which *of you,* if a sheep was lost, would not find it? Perhaps beyond the circle of inquiring, critical Pharisees were some women listening. Or what woman, had she lost a piece

[ *67* ]

of silver, would not try to find it by searching? Then He told the story of the younger son, ending with the picture of the elder son, out of sympathy with his father's heart, and unable to welcome the sinning brother home. The criticism of the Pharisees has been transmuted by this parabolic answer of Jesus into the Gospel for the world.

The relation of these three parts of the one parable is evident. Here are the points of unity, the lost things, the sheep, the piece of silver, and the son. The found things: the sheep was found and brought back to the fold, the lost drachma was found and brought back to currency and purchasing power, the lost son was found and brought back to home and to service.

There is yet another link between the three phases. It is that of joy, joy in the presence of the angels, joy in heaven, and then, as though the final joy could not be expressed in the terminology of the eternal spaces, He borrowed the figurative language with which every home is familiar, "Let us make merry." Jesus thus made God speak in simplest speech that man might more easily believe. The three are unified by joy.

The three are seen to be one if we dwell on their differences. The first two give us the picture of the seeking of the lost things by the one who has lost them. The third gives us the picture of the lost son seeking home again. I love this parable because in it both Arminians and Calvinists are at home. The Calvinist will lay emphasis on the first two parts. The sheep made no motion towards home. It had to be found and carried home. The lost piece of silver could not find itself. The woman had to search and find it. The Arminian will lay the emphasis on the third part. The son had to come back before he was received. I am both Arminian and Calvinist, because I live in this parable. There can be no movement back home until God takes the first step towards finding. There can be no getting back home until there is response and return. In the diversities also we have a revelation of the spiritual unity of the teaching.

We are constrained to go further and inquire, Why are there three phases? What did our Lord mean by grouping the three pictures? There is no question whatever in the minds of expositors as to the suggestiveness of the first picture or of the last. The picture of the shepherd is so evidently the picture of the work of the Lord Himself, and the picture of the father is certainly an unveiling of the heart of God, and of His attitude toward returning men. The picture of the woman, on the other hand, presents a phase very often passed over carelessly in modern exposition. Is this second picture a mere repetition of the first? Are the facts which our Lord would emphasize in the second the same as those He would emphasize in the first? Personally, I think not. I think there is as distinct and separate a value in the second phase as there is in the first, and as there surely is in the last. One of the most scholarly and devout expositors and theologians in lectures to lay preachers has solemnly warned them against fantastic interpretations, and has cited as fantastic the view that the first phase of this parable deals with the work of the Son, the second with that of the Spirit, and the third with that of the Father. In spite of that warning, I emphatically adopt that as my view, preferring the interpretations of some of the older expositors. Ambrose and Origen held that here, in the mind of the Master, was the thought of the action of the whole Godhead, that of Trinity in unity. Bengel, Alford, and Stier alike say that in the central picture we have a revelation of the peculiar activity of the Holy Spirit in His business of seeking lost things. Ambrose, Wordsworth and Oslhausen say that in the central picture we have the revelation of the responsibility of the

Church in its cooperation for the seeking of lost things. One at least, Oosterzee, has said that at the heart of the parable we have both these ideas, the revelation of the activity and responsibility of the Church in the power and presence of the Holy Spirit. I adopt that view, believing that in this parable we have the unification of the truth of God's attitude toward the lost. For our human seeing and understanding He broke up that activity and revealed the threefold process. First, that of the shepherd, His own work specifically. Then that of the Spirit, searching in and through the Church. Finally, that of the father, welcoming home the prodigal.

Let us look at these first two phases a little more carefully. First, the picture of the Shepherd, or the Son, seeking the lost sheep. We must remember the purpose of the picture—these Pharisees with their criticism and misunderstanding of Jesus, and their condemnation of His attitude. It was in answer to their criticism He was speaking. Why should Jesus have been at such pains to answer the criticism of these men? Not, as I understand it, for their sakes merely, but because He knew that through the ages Pharisees and scribes would continue. He knew that to the end, in the midst of organized religion, there would still be the attitude of the Pharisees and scribes, resulting from ignorance of the Word of God and inability to appreciate the value of sinning men. So, keeping the Pharisees and scribes in mind, we can use them as mirrors, in order to discover what God thinks of such attitude, whether in them or in us.

In the first phase of the parable we find a value missing from the second and third phases. It has been said that if we accept the parable of the prodigal son as revealing the attitude and activity of God for men, we have to omit a great many things that we have held to be of vast importance in the Christian Church. But we do not admit that the parable of the prodigal son supplies all the facts. It is an unveiling only of one phase. It is not the parable of the prodigal son, as we have already said. It is the parable of the father's heart. In this first picture I find something missing in the last. In that there are two sons, the younger and the elder. The younger took his portion and squandered it in the far country. The elder stayed at home and did his duty. Forgetting for the moment the supreme value of that picture, that of the revelation of the Father, look only at the sons. Neither son is perfect. The younger son was a disastrous failure. The elder son was equally a failure in other ways. So in the third picture we see a perfect father without a perfect son. Going back to the first phase, we find the missing Son; not the younger, not the elder, but the First-born, the Only Begotten, veiling Himself behind the sweet and tender imagery of the shepherd-lover of the lost sheep. We cannot interpret the parable apart from the One who spoke it. Believing as we do that when He spoke of that shepherd seeking, finding, and rejoicing He was speaking out of His own heart, we find that thus the parable is completed. Here is the true Son who never took His portion and went to the far country, the Son who was in such sympathy with the Father that He went after the wanderer to seek and restore him; the first-born Son, the Only-begotten of the Father. That is the first value of the first phase.

Notice the method of the parable, the introductory words. "What man of you?" Jesus was evidently defending His action by appealing to His hearers, putting them in His place as it were, but on a much lower level. "What man of you, having a hundred sheep, and having lost one of them, doth not leave the ninety and nine in the wilderness, and go after that which is lost, until he find it? And when he hath found it, he layeth it on his shoulders, rejoicing." What is the motive our Lord suggested? We take this little picture, and the heart is stirred by it. We talk and sing of its compassion. No audience can be unmoved when we sing,

"There were ninety and nine that safely lay
    In the shelter of the fold.
But one was out on the hills away,
    Far off from the gates of gold—
Away on the mountains wild and bare,
    Away from the tender Shepherd's care."

The spirit of the Christian Church has interpreted the story accurately, but there is no touch or word of compassion as Jesus uttered the parable. He did not say anything about compassion. The motive to which He was appealing in the hearts of these men was not that of compassion. What then was the motive? The value of the lost sheep. This question of Jesus made an entirely commercial suggestion. What man of you having lost a sheep would not go to find it, not because of compassion, but because of the value of the sheep?

Thus the Lord rebuked the contempt of these Pharisees for sinning men. There they stood, scribes and Pharisees, with the phylacteries on brow and around the border of the garment, gathering their robes around them lest they should be contaminated by these sinning men, and criticizing Him for getting so near to them. He said they had no right to hold these men in contempt. If *you* had lost a *sheep*—! But are not these goats? Nothing of the kind. They are sheep. But they might have said, Surely you do not mean to say that these men are valuable! That is the supreme thing He did mean. If you have gathered your garments about you lest you should be contaminated by touching some sinning man, imagining him to be of less value than you are, the first content of this parable is this: I am here because these are sheep of my Father's flock. What man of you, on the basis of your commercialism, would not leave the ninety and nine and go after the one?

Yet there is more in it than that. The method of the Master's figure is that of similarity and disparity. As though He had said, I am here sitting among these men and eating with them, and gathering them familiarly to my heart, first, because of their value, and, second, because of my love for them. The value of the sheep and the compassion of the Shepherd constitute the motive of the work of the Son. The Church has caught the last significance, and rightly caught it, and expressed it in hymn and song. Do not let us miss the other.

What, then, is the teaching of that phase of the parable indirectly? As to the sheep, that they are the property of God, and that all men are valuable to God. Preacher, teacher, worker in the slum area must cancel all such words as *worthless* if they are going to work with this Christ. Do not let us hear any more about these worthless people. Do not imagine that sin can make a man worthless to God. *"My sheep."*

As to the shepherd, what is the revelation? That the sheep is lost to Him, and lost to the flock, and lost to the fulness of His intention. The supreme revelation is that the Shepherd cares, that the Shepherd acts even at cost, that the Shepherd succeeds, and that the Shepherd rejoices—and I find a touch of tender sarcasm here—rejoices more over one than over the ninety and nine that needed no such seeking.

The direct teaching of the first phase is that of the joy of heaven over the restoration of lost sheep, and the consequent criticism of that attitude that sees no value in the lost, the degraded, and the debased. Degraded, utterly so; debased, unquestionably so; but worth leaving heaven to find. It is a long journey over the mountains! It is the fight with the wolf! That is the suggestion of that first phase.

Glance briefly at the second phase, the

lost piece of silver. The figure is changed, but the underlying thought remains the same. It has been said that this is unworthy of the sweep of the parable, for the lost piece of silver was of no intrinsic value. Is not that the very point? Was there not fine satire in thus coming down to the lower level, only one piece of silver? Men might say, That is just it, only one little piece of silver, that is about the value of this man. The other nine are the same value each. The nine are not lost. One is lost. Take an upright, dignified Pharisee and put him beside a publican, each one a piece of silver. That one is of as great value as this one. Here is one great value of the parable to my heart—the value of lost things to God!

Look at the person introduced here—a woman. Stier says, "The Spirit is presented in Scripture from Genesis i.1.2, and downwards, as feminine and motherly." Scripture recognises the Motherhood of God. I say that with great reverence, and with profound conviction. We have not read the Bible accurately if we have found only the Fatherhood of God. I take one isolated instance to prove the statement. "As one whom his mother comforteth, so will I comfort you." We have no more right to leave that out of reckoning than

[ 77 ]

## The Parable of the Father's Heart

"Like as a father pitieth his children,
So the Lord pitieth them that fear him."

Jesus said something that appals me most for its tenderness, and the marvelous matchlessness of His grace. Standing on the slopes of the mountain, looking out over the doomed city of Jerusalem that He loved so well, He cursed the city, but how did He do it? Through tears, and with a voice tremulous with emotion in its unveiling of His own attitude. "O Jerusalem, Jerusalem, which killeth the prophets, and stoneth them that are sent unto her! how often would I have gathered thy children together, even as a hen gathereth her chickens under her wings, and ye would not!"

Throughout the Bible this Motherliness of God is presented, and in a most singular way the Spirit of God suggests that side of the unbroken unity of the Divine nature. Or again to quote the words of Stier, "The Spirit is present in Scripture, from Genesis i.1.2, downwards, as feminine and motherly." Yes, but surely there is more here than that. Is not the Church for evermore the bride? And is not that a beautiful phrase that the Free Churches have so largely dropped out of their vocabulary—Mother Church? I will not hand over that phrase to any

one section of the Church. I am quite willing
all should share it, but I claim a part of it—
Mother Church. There is suggestiveness in it.
The Church is Mother Church only as she is
Spirit-filled. All her motherliness passes away
when she is devoid of the presence of the Spirit
of God. All the wooing, winsome tenderness of
the Church of God is absent when the Spirit of
God is absent. To show the Divine activity,
Mother must be in the midst, the Motherhood
of God.

Again, Stier has said, "It is not the Holy
Ghost as He is a hypostasis in the depths of the
Godhead, but as He hath built for Himself a
house upon earth, and obtained for Himself a
possession." The thought of Stier is the picture
of the Spirit working through the Church. Here
is a woman looking for a lost coin, a coin with an
image and superscription. We are always safe in
interpreting a figure employed by Jesus in one
place by His figure of speech in another. A coin
with an image and superscription belongs to the
sovereign, the lord of the realm, and a woman
is seen searching for that coin.

In Dr. Burton's volume on Luke in the
Expositors' Bible he makes a suggestion full of
beauty, that the lost piece was one of the ten
that constituted the frontlet worn by a woman,

which was presented to her in the hour of her marriage. Somehow, this piece had become loosened, and she had lost it, and was seeking for it, not merely because of its intrinsic worth, but because of all that it said to her concerning the sacred relationship of marriage. In all likelihood that is the exact and accurate explanation of this phase of the Lord's parable. Thus with matchless grace the Lord revealed the Spirit working through His bride, and what is she doing? Three words tell us, all of them suggestive—lighting, sweeping, seeking. The emphasis here is on the importance of the quest, not pre-eminently on the value of the thing lost, nor on the suffering by which the lost thing can be found, nor even on the gladness of the heart of God when the lost thing is found. The emphasis is on the importance of the quest. The rejoicing is the result of the quest.

Silvester Horne took as the motto of his mission at Whitefields, "No quest, no conquest." Here is the quest. What is the conquest? The finding of the lost piece. When the woman says, Rejoice with me, she uses the same expression that the shepherd used when he had found the lost sheep. Bengel says that particular Greek word for *rejoice* is used exclusively of the Holy Spirit in Scripture. Wherever that word is used, it is employed by one writing, or speaking, in fellowship with the Holy Spirit.

This, then, is the picture of the Church doing her work in the fulness of the Spirit. Once again, here are the scribes and Pharisees who are saying, This is a terrible business. He is eating with publicans and sinners. He says, No, I am looking for God's lost coin. His image is on it still, though it is in the dust. I am doing something which is preparing the way for the great ministry of God's motherhood through the Church. Then He reaches the heart of it all, and reveals the love of God in the picture of the Father.

The exposition needs application. Where are we? How far have we entered into fellowship with Him in His view of the value of lost things? How far have we ever come into fellowship with Him in His suffering to save them, and His persistent seeking for them, and His joy when they come home again?

# VI

## AN APPEAL

*Wherefore, my beloved brethren, be ye stedfast, un-moveable, always abounding in the work of the Lord, forasmuch as ye know that your labour is not vain in the Lord.*—I.CORINTHIANS xv.58.

THE apostolic injunction comes with great force in these days of strenuous life, and of need for earnest endeavor. It charges us to forget the things which are behind, and to press forward towards the goal, the completion, the final victory. These words remind us of that perpetual vocation which admits of no vacation, "Wherefore, my beloved brethren, be ye stedfast, unmoveable, always abounding in the work of our Lord, forasmuch as we ye know that your labour is not vain in the Lord."

To understand the meaning of that statement, let us see its setting in this letter. It has been objected by some that these words, occurring at this point, seem to be of the nature of an anticlimax, for immediately preceding them is that great and wonderful challenge, "O death, where is thy victory? O death, where is thy sting?

[ *82* ]

The sting of death is sin; and the power of sin is the law; but thanks be to God, which giveth us the victory through our Lord Jesus Christ." Immediately following that, apparently separated from it, or having but little connection with it, is this sternly practical word of admonition, "Wherefore, my beloved brethren, be ye stedfast, unmoveable, always abounding in the work of the Lord, forasmuch as ye know that your labour is not vain in the Lord." Personally, I do not feel that this injunction is of the nature of an anticlimax, even though read in close and immediate connection with the challenge to death. It is when we have come into such close, immediate fellowship with Jesus Christ as to know the triumph of His victory over death that we are prepared for all the pathway of suffering service that stretches before us, and are equipped for the fulfilment of this injunction.

The word *wherefore* with which the text commences is related not merely to the words immediately preceding it. It is a habit from which we are suffering today of taking a text, looking at it by itself alone, or in relation only to the text immediately preceding it. I inquire on what argument does that *wherefore* base the appeal of the text? Not on the section immediately preceding, but on a verse in the very first chapter of the letter. In that chapter we have

the apostle's introduction of himself and ex-
hortation to his readers. Eight verses are thus
occupied. Then, in the ninth verse, there is a
fundamental affirmation, "God is faithful,
through whom ye were called into the fellowship
of his Son Jesus Christ our Lord." "Wherefore,"
because God is faithful who has put you into
partnership with Jesus Christ, "be ye stedfast,
unmoveable, always abounding in the work of
the Lord."

All that lies between the fundamental
affirmation and the final appeal might be sum-
marized, for the purpose of our study, in this
brief declaration. The apostle teaches that the
Church commissioned for work is hindered from
doing of her work by all the things of the carnal
life—divisions, lack of discipline, derelictions and
disputes—and he shows that the Church is
equipped for the doing of her work by the
spiritualities, recognition of the government of
the Spirit in the Church, obedience to the supreme law of love, and work inspired by the
vision of the Lord's victory and resurrection.
Having rebuked the carnalities, and revealed
the spiritualities, the apostle says, "Wherefore,
my beloved brethren, be ye stedfast, unmoveable,
always abounding in the work of the Lord."

The text, therefore, is a spacious one indeed, and the only way to come to an under-

standing of its message is by taking its simplest thoughts and attending to them alone. What is the central word of this text? "Be ye . . . in the work of the Lord." That is an appeal to the will, the appeal of the writer to the central citadel of human life. The apostle introduced that appeal by an appeal to the intellect, "Wherefore." That is always the word of the intellect. He based his appeal to the will on the brethren's understanding of the fundamental truths with which he had been dealing. He ended by an appeal to the emotion, "Forasmuch as ye know that your labour is not vain in the Lord." Like so many of the apostolic appeals, this is an appeal to the whole life. Paul approached the central citadel, the will, along the avenue of the intellect, "Wherefore," and the massive arguments preceding are in mind. He ended by appealing once more to the will through the emotion as he gave one glimpse of the joy, the crown, the glory resulting from service. At the heart of everything is the appeal to the will, "Be ye . . . in the work of the Lord."

We inquire, then, What is the work of the Lord? for in answering that inquiry we shall be led to understand what is the work of the Christian Church. The sublimest meaning of this text lies on its surface. We who bear the name and wear the sign of Christ are charged not to initiate new movements or discover new methods, or endeavor in any way to help God. We are charged to be "in the work of the Lord." To understand our work, therefore, we must understand His work. I reverently affirm that Christ's work in London is our work in London. We shall understand what our work is by understanding what His work is. We cancel the past tense in our reference to Him, remembering He is "the same yesterday, today, and forever." If we may see Him at work in the olden days we shall understand His work today, and therefore our work today. I shall attempt to look at His work in the olden days in no way other than by receiving from His own lips explanation thereof in definition and declaration. I propose to cite three instances in which He did most clearly defend or define His work in answer to the criticism of His enemies.

Three occasions come to mind. At the commencement of His public ministry, John records how Jesus passed through Bethesda's porches and healed an impotent man. When they criticized Him for breaking the Sabbath in beneficent work, He answered them in these words, "My Father worketh hitherto, and I work." Later in His ministry He was seen, to the astonishment of those who beheld Him, to go in to lodge with a man who was a sinner,

Zacchæus the publican. When they criticized
Him for the action, He answered in those mem-
orable words, "The Son of man came to seek
and to save that which was lost." When the
scribes and Pharasees murmured against Him
because He received and ate with publicans and
sinners He answered in our one matchless parable in its three phases of revelation in Luke xv.

They charged Him with breaking the
Sabbath when He healed the impotent man, and
He replied, "My Father worketh hitherto, and I
work," an almost strangely significant declaration. They said to Him, Thou hast broken
Sabbath by healing this man. He said, in effect,
God can have no Sabbath in the presence of
human limitation and suffering. "My Father
worketh hitherto, and I work." The work of
God and the work of Christ, continuous and
one, was revealed in that sentence to be work
born of the Divine discontent in the presence
of human suffering and limitation. It is as
though Jesus had said to His critics on that occasion, Sabbath! God can have no Sabbath while
men are in this condition. God will forfeit His
Sabbath rights in order to make Sabbaths for
such men as these. That is the work of the Lord.
It is work that sets aside the inalienable, personal rights of God in order to correct and
negative and destroy the destructive forces in

the world, and bring man back into possession of his lost rights.

To take the second of these words: "The Son of man is come to seek and to save that which is lost." While the first declaration is that He is in union with His Father in work, the second makes a little more clear what that work is. He came to seek and to save that which was lost. There is no need to stay with an exposition of that, but pass at once to the explanatory parable, with which we have already dealt in our previous study. The teaching may be crystallized by saying that the Church is in the work of the Lord in the proportion in which she suffers with the Son, searches diligently with the Spirit, and is able to sing with the Father when the wanderer returns.

How much do we really know of what it is to suffer with the Son for the salvation of the lost? How much have we, who bear the name and sign of our adorable Lord, ever entered into actual fellowship with His sufferings in seeking and saving the lost? It is one thing to sing of suffering; it is quite another to suffer. It is one thing to meditate in the presence of His suffering until the very stigmata appear in the palms of our hands; but it is quite another to know the fellowship of His suffering. How many journeys have we ever taken over the steep and precipitous mountains and through lonely valleys to find one lost sheep? What do we really know of blood and sacrifice in our endeavor to save men? What do we know of the zeal of the house of the Lord which consumes? My own sad but profound conviction is that the Church of God is trifling with her work. I am not uttering censorious criticism. I know how much of sacred sacrifice there is in the lives of individual saints. But take the great Church as a whole, how many know anything of what it is to be in the actual business of seeking and saving men through labor that means pain and weariness, wounds and suffering? We cannot be in the work of the Lord while we touch the work with dainty, distant fingers. A check out of superabundance is worth nothing until it is accompanied by our own personal sacrificial service.

Suffering with the Son! We are familiar with it: the picture which our painters have painted and our poets have wrought into songs that we can never sing without feeling the thrill of His passion and the movement of His tender sacrificial love. But let us honestly inquire how much do we know of the perilous journey and the sacrificial service. Being in the work of the Lord means being in partnership with Him in the suffering that is involved in seeking and saving.

*The Parable of the Father's Heart*

We must also know the diligence of the woman who kindled a light, and swept, and sought until she found. I know how difficult it is, how easy it is to say of some case, a man in the congregation, a youth in the class, a girl or boy in the school, I am out of all patience with them. They are hopeless. Nay, verily. The woman sought until she found! That is the note we need to have impressed on our hearts, the diligent, persistent search until the victory is won.

To pass to the last phase of the parable. If we are in the work of the Lord there must be not only suffering with the Son, searching with the Spirit, the diligent quest that knows no rest until the lost be found; we must also be able to sing with the Father when the prodigal comes home. I think this last is what the Church least realizes. Can you be merry with God if the prodigal comes home to you? Would you feel great gladness in your heart if there strayed into your pew a man in rags? This is the test for the Christian Church.

So we come back to the fundamental truth. The foundation for all Christian service is a superabundant conviction of the value to God of every human life. Pause on your way and look straight into the most degraded face you meet, and remember that soul is as dear to God as you are. If we can come to feel this, and

[ *90* ]

know it; if it can become part of our very life, then we shall sing when that soul comes home, and count contact with defilement as a precious thing if it means that we are helping that one back to purity and to God?

"Be . . . in the work of the Lord." We can be in the work of the Lord only as we are prepared for the toilsome journey that involves weariness and suffering and conflict. We can be in the work of the Lord only as we catch the spirit of His unwearying patience in seeking for the lost. We can be in the work of the Lord only as His love is so shed abroad in our hearts that we shall in very deed welcome to heart and home and sanctuary the prodigal in rags and defilement, bringing such a one back to the robe, the ring, and the sandals of the Father's house.

Note the words that the apostle used to describe our attitude, or relation to this work, "stedfast, unmoveable, always abounding in the work of the Lord." There is no redundancy of words here. No single one is useless. Each has a different significance. "Stedfast," that suggests settled constancy in work. "Unmoveable" suggests constancy as against opposition. That worker for God is the honored one who is characterized by fidelity. Sometimes I think there are Christians who will never get to heaven unless they die in a revival, for only then are they active.

Others I know who are always in their places, Sabbath by Sabbath, with the boys and girls around them in the school. Their work is not noticed in the religious press. On that account they are to be congratulated, did they but know it. There is no flourish of trumpets, but quiet, persistent toil. They are "unmoveable" as against all the suggestion of the evil one, as against all the enticements of the world, the flesh, and the devil.

How they tried to move the Lord from His high purpose! How the devil tried with insidious temptation! How His friends tried with mistaken affection! How His mother tried to persuade Him to go home because He was overworking Himself! There is an affinity closer than that of blood relationship. In the spiritual world those are kin of Christ who do the will of God.

"Always abounding." I translate that *always* literally, and it is *everywhen*. I interpret the Greek word for *abounding* by its use in another connection. When Christ fed the multitude they gathered up that which *remained over*. That is the same Greek word. Our service is to be service in which there is that which remains over. There is no room for cynical prudence and foot-rules and balances here. "Always abounding!" That is a vocation which admits of no vacation. Do not misunderstand that. It is necessary, in the interests of work, to have vacations, but we may still fulfil vocation in vacation. "Always abounding." Wherever we come into contact in religious services or in recreative life with a lost man or woman, there is our opportunity. "Always abounding."

We conclude as my text ends, "Forasmuch as ye know that your labour is not in vain in the Lord." The sacrificial journey results in the finding of the lost sheep. The diligent search in the house results in the finding of the lost piece of silver. The overwhelming passion of the father's heart wings its way over the far distances, and sings its song in the heart of the prodigal in the day of famine, and the prodigal answers it, and finds his way home, and the father is merry. "Your labour is not in vain in the Lord." By which the apostle meant to say that the reward of service is the success of service.

When John wrote his letter to the elect lady he said, "I rejoice greatly that I have found certain of thy children walking in the truth." That was his joy when he wrote to Gaius, and said, "Greater joy have I none than this, to hear of my children walking in the truth." When the great apostle wrote to others, he said, "What is our hope, or joy, or crown of glorying? Are not even ye before our Lord Jesus at his coming?

For ye are our glory and joy." Not only in the heaven that lies beyond is there reward for service. Take one long journey over the mountains, a journey that costs something, and get your arms about some lost sheep of the fold, and you will have your reward there and then. Be diligent, and sweep, until there flashes from the dust the glitter of the lost piece of silver, and you will have joy and a reward. Let us drop these figures of speech. Have you ever been the means of saying some word that has brought a soul to Christ? Then you have had your reward. The reward of service is in its success, and the proportion in which the toiling and seeking are answered by the singing is the proportion in which already we are entering into the joy.

Yet the fulness of it all lies beyond. There are some strange things sung in revival meetings. I have heard people sing with a most curious lilt,

"Will anyone, then, at the Beautiful Gate
Be waiting and watching for me?"

I am not sure that the idea is theologically correct, but in the philosophy of Christian service it is true. If I would lay up reward in heaven, I must do it by toil on earth. I think even in heaven there will be the consciousness of imperfection unless I take with me someone else.

The reward of service, what is it? "Your

labour is not in vain." It is our victory that is
our reward. It is the sheep put down with the
others in the fold that is the reward for the
journeying. It is the piece of silver flashing
again, perchance, in the frontlet of the bride's
forehead that is the reward which makes her
heart glad. It is the boy at home that fills the
father's heart with merriment.

In the present victory of sacrificial service
there is ample reward, yet God in grace had laid
up a far more wonderful reward. All these
things shall be found in the day that has no sun-
set. Our wealth in heaven will not be the wealth
of harps provided, or crown worn, but of the
souls we have led to Christ and to God. "Forasmuch as ye know that your labour is not vain in
the Lord."

The way of victory is the way of *labor*.
Earth is the only place for that. We shall not
end our work when we go to heaven, but we
shall end our *labor*. The great word of Revelation, so often misquoted, teaches that "they do
cease from their labour, but their works do go
out with them." The joy of it, the spaciousness
of it! The loved ones who have passed beyond
are still serving, but they have ceased from labor.
We can enter into the work of the Lord in this
world only by labor, by sacrificial toil. He ceased
from His labor when He ascended on high, but

[*95*]

## The Parable of the Father's Heart

not from His work. His work is still going forward. It is only by labor here that the great victory of God in the universe is won. "Your labour is not in vain in the Lord."

No man or woman who shares the Christ-life is free from responsibility, or is exempted from this high and holy privilege. God help us to understand our responsibility, our privilege. God help us to be in the work of the Lord, not watching it, not criticizing it, not applauding it, but in it; in our own flesh bearing the weariness, in our own mental consecration persisting patiently in seeking, in our own deepest spirit-life forever ready with the song as the prodigal comes home.

May God in His grace forgive the poverty of the interpretation, and bring us anew face to face with His own thought and purpose, and send us forth as never before, "stedfast, unmoveable, always abounding in the work of the Lord."